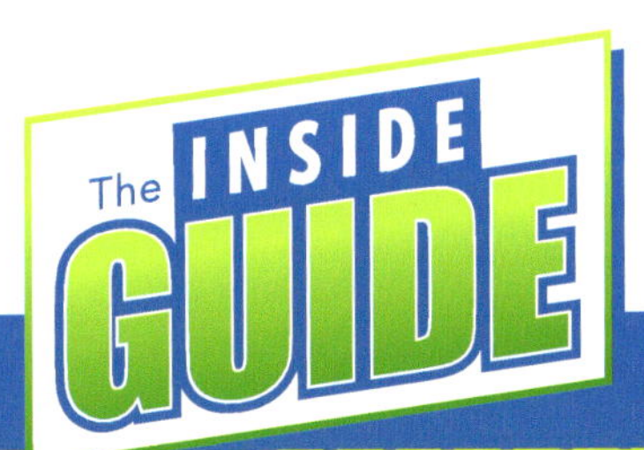

CIVIL RIGHTS HEROES

Coretta Scott King

By Cassie M. Lawton

New York

Published in 2022 by Cavendish Square Publishing, LLC
29 E. 21st Street, New York, NY 10010

First Edition

Website: cavendishsq.com

Portions of this work were originally authored by Maria Nelson and published as *Coretta Scott King (Civil Rights Crusaders)*. All new material this edition authored by Cassie M. Lawton.

Library of Congress Cataloging-in-Publication Data
Names: Lawton, Cassie M., author.
Title: Coretta Scott King / Cassie M. Lawton.
Description: New York : Cavendish Square Publishing, [2022] | Series: The inside guide: Civil Rights heroes | Includes bibliographical references and index.
Identifiers: LCCN 2020027269 | ISBN 9781502660046 (library binding) | ISBN 9781502660022 (paperback) | ISBN 9781502660039 (set) | ISBN 9781502660053 (ebook)
Subjects: LCSH: King, Coretta Scott, 1927-2006–Juvenile literature. | African American women civil rights workers–Biography–Juvenile literature. | Civil rights–United States–History–Juvenile literature.
Classification: LCC E185.97.K47 L39 2022 | DDC 323.092 [B]–dc23
LC record available at https://lccn.loc.gov/2020027269

Editor: Kristen Susienka
Copy Editor: Abby Young
Designer: Andrea Davison-Bartolotta

The photographs in this book are used by permission and through the courtesy of: Cover Pix Inc./The LIFE Picture Collection via Getty Images; p. 4 Photo12/UIG/Getty Images; p. 6 CNP/Hulton Archive/Getty Images; p. 7 SDI Productions/E+/Getty Images; pp. 8, 16, 20, 25, 28 (top left) Bettmann/Getty Images; p. 9 Allison Silberberg/Getty Images; p. 10 FrankRamspott/iStock/Getty Images Plus/Getty Images; p. 11 Julian Brown/The Boston Globe via Getty Images; p. 12 (top) Tetra Images/Getty Images; pp. 12 (bottom), 14 Michael Ochs Archives/Getty Images; p. 13 Kruck20/iStock/Getty Images Plus/Getty Images; pp. 15, 18 Grey Villet/The LIFE Picture Collection via Getty Images; p. 19 The Abbott Sengstacke Family Papers/Robert Abbott Sengstacke/Getty Images; p. 21 Moneta Sleet Jr./UPI/Bettmann/Getty Images; p. 22 Erik S. Lesser/Liasion Agency/Hulton Archive/Getty Images; p. 24 Paras Griffin/Getty Images; p. 26 Paul Almasy/Corbis/VCG via Getty Images; p. 28 (bottom left) J. Wilds/Keystone/Hulton Archive/Getty Images; p. 28 (top right) Keystone View Company/Archive Photos/Getty Images; p. 28 (bottom right) Spencer Platt/Getty Images; p. 29 (top) Filippo Monteforte/AFP via Getty Images; p. 29 (bottom) Justin Sullivan/Getty Images.

CPSIA compliance information: Batch #CS22CSQ: For further information contact Cavendish Square Publishing LLC, New York, New York, at 1-877-980-4450.

Printed in the United States of America

CONTENTS

Coretta Scott King was more than the wife of Dr. Martin Luther King Jr. Her actions inspired many.

WHO WAS CORETTA SCOTT KING?

Coretta Scott King was a brave **civil rights** leader. She lived during a time of great change in America. This time of change was called the civil rights movement.

The Wife of a King

Many people know Coretta as the wife of Dr. Martin Luther King Jr. He was one of the most important leaders of the civil rights movement. He gave speeches all around the country and walked in marches for civil rights. He was known as as a nonviolent man. He always tried to help others, especially the African American community.

Working Together

Together, Coretta Scott King and her husband worked hard to help Black Americans gain rights. These included the right to vote, which was something not everyone could do because of **discriminating** treatment by people in power. African Americans living in the southern United States had a particularly hard time voting. Coretta and Martin worked hard to gain voting rights for everyone in those communities.

Martin Luther King Jr. led the civil rights movement in the 1950s and 1960s.

Fast Fact

Martin gave many speeches. He gave his "I Have a Dream" speech to more than 250,000 people in Washington, D.C., in 1963.

A Life Apart

Coretta worked for justice in the 1950s and 1960s. During this time, Black Americans living in the South faced many challenges. Jim Crow laws, which separated Black people from white people, divided cities and towns. Black and white Americans visited different restaurants, movie theaters, and grocery stores. They drank at different water fountains. Kids went to different schools. The separate facilities for Black Americans were often of a lower quality. This kind of separation was called segregation.

The civil rights movement helped gain rights, such as voting rights, for African Americans in the United States.

THE CIVIL RIGHTS MOVEMENT

The civil rights movement began to gain national attention in 1955 when a woman named Rosa Parks refused to give up her seat on a city bus in Montgomery, Alabama. Back then, Black bus riders had to move to the back of the bus if the bus was crowded and a white person got on. Parks's action sparked a citywide bus **boycott** and the eventual end of segregated buses in Montgomery. Black **activists** worked hard to end segregation throughout America. They did so through speeches, marches, and other public forms of protest. Television helped call attention to the harsh ways Black Americans were treated, especially in the South, and led to more people calling for change.

Staying Strong

Segregation was a part of life for Coretta. She and her family lived in Alabama, which is a southern state. They were targets of discrimination and even of violence for fighting for their rights. However, they didn't let this stop them from helping others.

Fast Fact

Jim Crow was a character in a play. He was goofy and clumsy. His actions became a **stereotype** for all African Americans.

People in the South had to use different drinking fountains depending on whether they were Black or white.

Leaving a Mark

Later in her life, Coretta was a major influence on other movements for justice and equality. She gave speeches in favor of equal rights for women and peace all over the world. She stood up for those who were forgotten or mistreated. Coretta believed everyone should be listened to and respected, no matter who they were or what they looked like.

Fast Fact

In 1954, a court case called *Brown v. Board of Education of Topeka* said schools couldn't be segregated anymore.

Coretta Scott King lived a full life helping others.

Coretta was born in a small town in Alabama. This was one of the most segregated states at the time.
Alabama

GROWING UP AND WORKING HARD

Coretta Scott was born in the small town of Marion, Alabama, on April 27, 1927. At that time, Alabama was a very segregated state. Coretta's parents were **entrepreneurs**. Her mother liked to sing and play music. This inspired Coretta to become a musician later in life. Coretta was one of four children, and she worked hard to help her family.

Education

Coretta was smart and enjoyed learning. Her favorite subject was music. She loved to sing. She joined choirs in school and studied hard. She became one of her school's top students. She graduated first in her high school class from Lincoln Normal School in 1945. Then, she studied music at Antioch College in Yellow Springs, Ohio, and later at the New England Conservatory of Music in Boston, Massachusetts. That's where she met Martin Luther King Jr.

Coretta was a great singer. She studied music in college.

Martin was the son of a minister, or church leader, from Atlanta, Georgia. He was studying theology, or religion, at Boston University.

Fast Fact

The New England Conservatory of Music is America's oldest independent music conservatory, or school. It was started in 1867.

Falling in Love

Martin and Coretta didn't fall in love right away. It took some time to happen. Eventually, the two began to date. In 1953, they were married. The wedding was a big event—350 guests came!

Coretta was still studying in Boston when she got married. She graduated in 1954, and then, she and Martin moved to Montgomery, Alabama. There, Martin became a minister at the Dexter Avenue Baptist Church.

Fast Fact

The Dexter Avenue Baptist Church was a meeting place for activists. It was also bombed several times during the civil rights movement.

Coretta and Martin were a team. They worked together for social justice.

MONTGOMERY: A CENTER OF ACTIVISM

Montgomery, Alabama, played an important role in the history of the civil rights movement. It was the site of the Montgomery bus boycott. It then became the first Southern city to have its bus system desegregated. Soon after that, it became the place where many civil rights activists planned, prepared, and faced tough moments. In 1961, its bus station became the center of a fight between **Freedom Riders** and an angry mob of white citizens. It also was the final stop for marchers in 1965 who traveled from Selma, Alabama, to call for voting rights. Today, it has many landmarks and museums connected to the civil rights movement.

Today, Montgomery, Alabama's capital city, offers many opportunities to learn about the civil rights movement.

Family Life

Coretta and Martin had four children. Yolanda was born in 1955 and Martin III in 1957. Later came Dexter, born in 1961, then Bernice, in 1963.

Martin wanted Coretta to stay home and care for the children, but that didn't stop her. She was determined to help others, just like her husband. The couple traveled the world together. They saw poor people in Mexico and visited India to learn about Indian peacemaker Mahatma Gandhi. These trips had a great impact on Coretta.

Fast Fact

Mahatma Gandhi was a leader who used peace to make changes. His actions and thoughts inspired Martin Luther King Jr., although they never met.

Coretta (*center*) was a caring mother to her four children, but she also worked hard outside the home during the civil rights movement.

A Change

In 1955, the world was starting to change. Black Americans in the South weren't happy with segregation. They wanted a different life. They wanted to use the same facilities as white people. They didn't want to be forced into separate spaces.

Martin and Coretta took part in the Montgomery bus boycott from 1955 to 1956. They became civil rights leaders in their community. Together, they motivated others through their actions and words.

Many people walked to work during the Montgomery bus boycott. In the end, this boycott was successful and helped other cities around the country become desegregated.

Coretta was her own person, not just one half of a married couple. She made sure people knew it through her actions and words.

CORETTA TAKING CHARGE

Coretta became one of the most well-known women of the civil rights movement and spoke out about the need to include more women in the movement. She supported her husband, but when she suddenly found herself without him, she also became a leader on her own.

Tough Times

Coretta spent much of the early days of the civil rights movement standing by Martin's side as he directed others and helped lead the movement in the South. Martin's work and Coretta's support of it sometimes put their lives in danger. In fact, their house was bombed in 1956 when Coretta was home with their daughter Yolanda. Coretta was lucky to be alive, but she didn't let this act of violence stop her from supporting her husband and standing by his side.

Fast Fact

Coretta planned and took part in "Freedom Concerts." These events raised money for the Southern Christian Leadership Conference—a civil rights group.

"Freedom Concerts," like this one in 1963, allowed people to come together for a good cause and enjoy music from popular performers.

Traveling

Coretta and Martin became popular figures. They traveled the world, sometimes together but sometimes apart. Coretta was often seen marching next to her husband at important protests during the civil rights movement. At other times, she watched the children while Martin traveled.

Coretta's Beliefs

Coretta had her own voice and her own beliefs. She was very much against war and for peace. Unlike Martin, Coretta spoke out early about her feelings toward a war that was starting in Vietnam. Later, she was asked to take part in international peace talks and events, such as the Women's Strike for Peace. She joined the Women's International League for Peace and Freedom in 1968. She also gave speeches when Martin couldn't.

Coretta joined her husband for marches and at other public events.

Martin's Death

On April 4, 1968, Coretta's world was turned upside down. That day, Martin was assassinated, or killed, at a motel in Memphis, Tennessee. Coretta was **devastated**, but she wouldn't let his death

Fast Fact

The Women's Strike for Peace was a worldwide event protesting **nuclear testing**. It happened on November 1, 1961.

stop her from working. Days after the tragedy, Coretta led and spoke at a march that Martin was supposed to join. Later, she spoke at the Lincoln Memorial in Washington, D.C., as part of the Poor People's Campaign. These actions made people respect Coretta for the activist she was. It also turned her into a new leader for the civil rights movement.

Coretta spoke at different gatherings, such as this one for the Poor People's Campaign in Washington, D.C., in 1968.

Taking Martin's Place

Coretta believed the country needed to change. At first, she used parts of Martin's famous speeches about racial equality when she spoke. Then, she figured out

Fast Fact

Other leaders were also killed in the 1960s, including activist Malcolm X and President John F. Kennedy.

her own message—she wanted everyone to be equal. Coretta spent the rest of her life working for civil rights for all, especially women. She kept Martin's **legacy** alive while also creating her own.

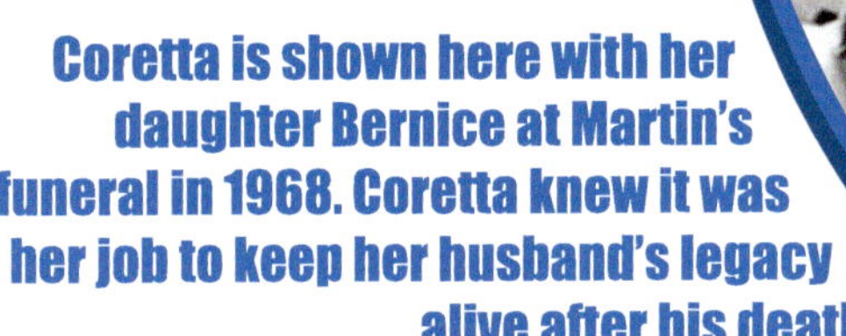

Coretta is shown here with her daughter Bernice at Martin's funeral in 1968. Coretta knew it was her job to keep her husband's legacy alive after his death.

THE CIVIL RIGHTS ACT

The civil rights movement led to real changes for Black Americans. The Civil Rights Act of 1964 made it illegal to discriminate against anyone based on race, beliefs, or whether they are a man or a woman. This also ended segregation in public places. This was an important step in the history of the civil rights movement. Martin, Coretta, and other activists worked hard to get the Civil Rights Act passed. The work of Martin, Coretta, and other activists also led to another important act, called the Voting Rights Act of 1965. This act stopped practices that kept Black people from voting.

Coretta continued helping others as she got older.

A LIFE WELL LIVED

Coretta made a decision to carry on Martin's dreams and mission. She did this in many ways: by writing books about her life with him, starting organizations devoted to his causes, and delivering speeches all over the world. However, she did more than just make sure people remembered Martin; she made sure they remembered her too.

Remembering Martin

In 1968, months after Martin died, Coretta started the Martin Luther King Jr. Center for Nonviolent Social Change in Atlanta. Today, it's known as the King Center. It educates people about taking peaceful actions during difficult times and about social justice. In 1969, Coretta published a book called *My Life with Martin Luther King, Jr.* In January 1986, she accomplished another goal of hers—to make Martin's birthday a national holiday.

> **Fast Fact**
>
> In 2017, Coretta's last book was published posthumously, or after she died. It's called *Coretta: My Life, My Love, My Legacy.*

The King Center in Atlanta is shown here.

Fast Fact

Martin Luther King Jr. Day is celebrated on the third Monday in January. People all around the country volunteer or attend events.

Her Own Work

Coretta also spent a lot of time working for equality for all. She believed all people deserved to be treated the same, no matter who they were or where they came from. She cared especially about equal rights for women and groups such as the poor and the **LGBTQ+** community. In the 1990s, she voiced support for the LGBTQ+ community, hoping that one day everyone could live in a world in which people loved and supported each other.

Coretta believed that women everywhere should be treated the same as men.

ENJOYING THE ARTS

Two prizes, one for authors and one for illustrators, are carrying on Coretta Scott King's name and legacy today. The Coretta Scott King Awards honor one African American author and one African American illustrator who've captured the African American experience in their work. Books selected focus on either young adult or children's audiences. The award for authors started in 1969, and the illustration award began in 1974. The 2020 award winner for authors was *New Kid* by Jerry Craft. That same year, *The Undefeated*, illustrated by Kadir Nelson, won the illustration award.

Coretta helped form many groups that fought for equality, including the Full Employment Action Council in 1974 to fight for jobs for the unemployed. She also met with peacemakers from all over the world, including presidents and other political leaders.

A Voice for Others

Coretta also stood up for the rights of people in other countries. For example, for many years in South Africa, there was another type of segregation

Every public place in South Africa was separated, including public benches.

happening called apartheid. This had been going on for decades, but an anti-apartheid movement was gaining more support in the 1980s. People in South African towns lived, worked, and played in areas separated by race. Coretta thought this segregation was wrong. She protested against it and was arrested.

Fast Fact

One of the biggest leaders against apartheid was Nelson Mandela. He was a South African activist who became the country's president.

A Long, Full Life

As she grew older, Coretta became more active in other issues in the United States. She spoke about civil rights and about economic issues. She also toured the country, wrote more books, and protected Martin's legacy. Above all, she continued to work hard. She died on January 30, 2006, having lived a full life working for justice. Today, the King family still continues the work of Coretta and Martin.

TIMELINE

In Coretta's Life | **In the World**

1927
Coretta Scott is born on April 27.

1929
The Great Depression starts.

1953
Coretta marries Martin Luther King Jr. on June 18.

1963
John F. Kennedy is assassinated.

1964
The Civil Rights Act passes.

1968
Martin is assassinated on April 4.

1969
My Life with Martin Luther King, Jr. is published.

1986
Martin Luther King Jr. Day becomes a national holiday.

2001
The September 11 terrorist attacks occur.

2006
Coretta Scott King dies on January 30.

THINK ABOUT IT!

1. Why are civil rights important in a society? What groups have had to fight for civil rights throughout history?

2. Think about Coretta's and Martin's approaches to social change. Do you think their message of nonviolence was the right way to bring change? Why or why not?

3. What changes do you think are needed in society today? How could you help start your own movement?

4. Did Coretta's story inspire you? What can you learn from her about making the world a better place for all people?

GLOSSARY

activist: A person who works to bring change in the world.

boycott: The act of refusing to have dealings with a person or business in order to force change.

civil right: A freedom granted to people by law.

devastate: To deeply sadden.

discriminate: To treat people differently because of race or beliefs.

entrepreneur: A person starting a business.

Freedom Rider: A person who traveled on buses to different states in the South in the 1960s, trying to change segregation laws dealing with buses and bus stations.

legacy: The memory or work of a person after they've died.

LGBTQ+: Relating to a group made up of people who see themselves as a gender different from the sex they were assigned at birth or who want to be in romantic relationships that aren't only male-female. LGBTQ stands for lesbian, gay, bisexual, transgender, and queer or questioning.

nuclear testing: The practice of dropping very powerful bombs in desert areas; these took place between the 1940s and 1970s.

stereotype: A way of thinking about a person or group of people based on certain characteristics or habits; stereotypes aren't always accurate and can be harmful.

FIND OUT MORE

Books

Calkhoven, Laurie. *Martin Luther King Jr.* New York, NY: DK, 2019.

Herman, Gail. *Who Was Coretta Scott King?* New York, NY: Penguin, 2017.

Hooks, Gwendolyn. *If You Were a Kid During the Civil Rights Movement.* New York, NY: Children's Press, 2017.

Websites

Civil Rights Movement
kids.britannica.com/kids/article/civil-rights-movement/403522
This website explores key moments and actions in the civil rights movement and includes a slideshow of historic photographs.

Fun Facts from Black History: Coretta Scott King
www.youtube.com/watch?v=Mr3P9vVo-ao
This short animated video for students explores the biography of Coretta Scott King.

Hero for All: Martin Luther King Jr.
kids.nationalgeographic.com/explore/history/martin-luther-king-jr
This website from *National Geographic Kids* presents facts about Martin Luther King Jr.'s life and legacy.

Publisher's note to educators and parents: Our editors have carefully reviewed these websites to ensure that they are suitable for students. Many websites change frequently, however, and we cannot guarantee that a site's future contents will continue to meet our high standards of quality and educational value. Be advised that students should be closely supervised whenever they access the Internet.

INDEX